THE GREINER GROWTH MODEL

Anticipate crises and adapt
to a changing business world

Written by Jean Blaise Mimbang
In collaboration with Brigitte Feys
Translated by Carly Probert

Business **50MINUTES.com**

50MINUTES.com

PROPEL
YOUR BUSINESS FORWARD!

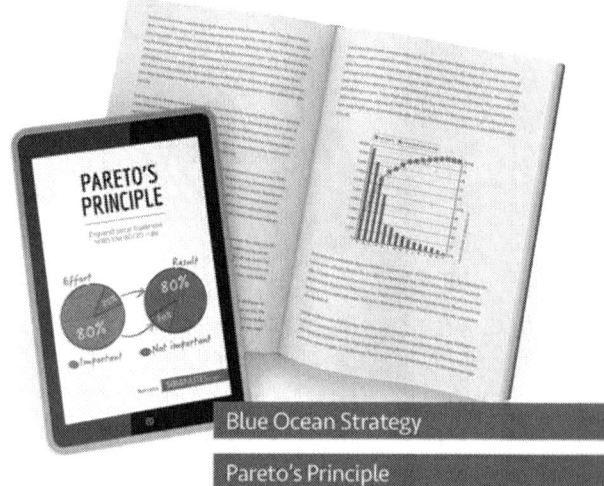

- Blue Ocean Strategy
- Pareto's Principle
- Managing Stress at Work
- Game Theory

www.50minutes.com

THE GREINER GROWTH MODEL FOR ORGANISATIONAL CHANGE   1

Key information
Introduction
History
Definition of the model

THEORY   5

Life cycles
Organisational change
Incremental approaches to the life cycle
Larry E. Greiner's Growth Model

LIMITATIONS AND EXTENSIONS   24

Limitations and criticisms
Related models and extensions

PRACTICAL APPLICATION: KODAK   27

Creativity phase
Direction phase
Delegation and coordination phase
Collaboration phase

SUMMARY   32

FURTHER READING   34

THE GREINER GROWTH MODEL FOR ORGANISATIONAL CHANGE

KEY INFORMATION

- **Names:** Greiner Growth Model, Greiner's model for organisational growth.
- **Uses:** Managing crises in a company, defining strategy and modelling organisational growth.
- **Why is it successful?**
    - The model is theoretically predictive. Depending on the company's sector of activity and changes in environmental factors, it allows users to locate and anticipate the next crisis (structural or functional change) that the organisation will have to deal with.
    - It allows users to identify certain indicators from the organisation's past that are critical to its future success.
    - It makes it easier to understand how fast-growing companies (startups) work.
- **Key words:**
    - <u>Organisational change:</u> The transformation process of the structure in a given context.
    - <u>Organisational life cycle:</u> All the phases, from creation to possible termination, through which a company passes.

INTRODUCTION

> "The history of any one part of the Earth, like the life of a soldier, consists of long periods of boredom and short periods of terror."

This quote from the British geologist Derek V. Ager, cited by Stephen Jay Gould (American palaeontologist, 1941-2002) in his book *The Panda's Thumb* (1982), could, by extension, be applied to humans and to businesses. Indeed, just like humans, companies are complex organisations that undergo various changes during their existence. These changes involve more or less significant periods of crisis which can threaten the very survival of the organisation.

In the face of the current economic reality of globalisation, all businesses must deal with the challenge of competitiveness. The companies that succeed in meeting this challenge are those that best manage and anticipate times of change and the next development phases of the company.

Depending on the organisation's sector of activity and on environmental factors, the model designed by Larry E. Greiner (American academic, born in 1933) allows a company to visualise what phase it is currently in and anticipate the next crisis it will have to face, in order to turn it into an opportunity for a new growth phase.

HISTORY

Theories related to organisational changes have been developed since the post-war period, and are compared and associated with the three major economic periods that have taken place since 1945 (Desreumaux, 1996).

- The first period began after the war and ended in the early 1970s. It corresponds to a phase of strong global economic growth, resulting in a system in equilibrium.
- The second period began with the start of the oil crises of the 1970s and lasted until the economic crisis of the early 1980s. It was during this phase, characterised by a high business mortality rate and significant organisational changes, that the Greiner Growth Model appeared in 1972.
- The third and final identifiable period extends from the early 1990s to the present day. The economic context of this phase of constant changes is characterised by turbulence and unpredictability.

DEFINITION OF THE MODEL

According to Larry E. Greiner, during its existence, a company goes through five well-defined growth phases interspersed with five key moments known as 'crises'. The transition from one phase to another is achieved through structural adaptations which mark the evolving nature of the organisational system.

The phases of change depend on the internal (age, size,

phases of growth and revolution, etc.) and external (competition, geographic location, industry growth rate, etc.) factors of the organisation. The five growth phases are:

- creativity;
- direction;
- delegation;
- coordination;
- collaboration.

These phases are potentially interspersed with five crises: leadership, autonomy, control, red tape and growth.

THEORY

LIFE CYCLES

In the same way that an organisation goes through phases of more or less significant changes that may jeopardise its survival over the course of its history, humans develop gradually over time, while undergoing periods of crisis which may bring about their demise.

Biological life cycle

The biological life cycle corresponds to the period of time during which the entire life of an organism takes place, starting with its conception. In general, the biological life cycle begins with birth, followed by a period of growth that leads to maturity, before an eventual period of decline, and, finally, death. Depending on the life cycle studied, the terminology is different, although the process remains comparable.

We can illustrate this using the example of the human biological life cycle:

- Conception is followed by birth and childhood. This is the 'launch period'.
- Then comes adolescence, characterised by the proliferation of different experiences within and outside of the family circle and corresponding to the phase called 'growth'. At this time, the human being constructs their personality as best they can through trial and error: they grow and acquire new knowledge and skills every day.

During this growth phase, they also discover their talents and weaknesses, which lead them to choose a profession, but also feelings and emotions, such as love. All this represents a positive change in their life.
- Finally, events that inhibit growth, such as retirement and old age, inevitably arise, marking the transition into the decline phase. This 'decay' leads to death, which is inevitable for all living organisms.

Business: a series of life cycles

At first glance, we may think that a company has only one life cycle. However, this is not at all the case. The company often finds itself at a crossroads, because it experiences many different life cycles, including material life cycles (product life cycle, technology life cycle or marketing life cycle), human and social life cycles (staff life cycle and organisation life cycle) and the life cycle of the business that it manages independently.

- The concept of the **product life cycle** is regularly used among marketing professionals, as each product follows its own life cycle. This cycle usually has four phases: launch, growth, maturity and decline. However, some analysts add a fifth phase, as before launching a product – like with embryonic development with humans – the company does market research, produces prototypes, etc. This additional phase is the development phase and aims to reduce the risk of failure during the launch of the product.
- **The commercial life cycle** is similar to the product life cycle, its only difference being that the fourth phase

corresponds to a potential re-launch.
- **The technology life cycle.** Like products, technology has its own life cycle that comprises four phases: early technology, emerging technology, key technology and core technology.
- **Staff life cycle.** With regards to staff, there is also a life cycle based on the careers of the individual employees. This cycle begins with recruitment, which is followed by growth (including training, promotion, etc.), maturity (at this point the employee is older, so it will be necessary to look for a replacement in the medium term) and ends with decline (dismissal, retirement, etc.).
- **Organisational or business life cycle**, which Greiner represents as a growth process in five phases.

ORGANISATIONAL CHANGE

As a reminder, organisational change is defined by reference to a given context or situation. It can also be defined in contrast to continuity.

Growth models

Theories concerning the pace of organisational change have evolved considerably since the late 1950s. To facilitate the analysis of the different structural typologies, we can look at the conclusions of Alain Desreumaux (French academic, born in 1944) in his 1996 book *Nouvelles formes d'organisation et évolution de l'entreprise* (*New Forms of Company Organisation and Evolution*).

Alain Desreumaux matrix

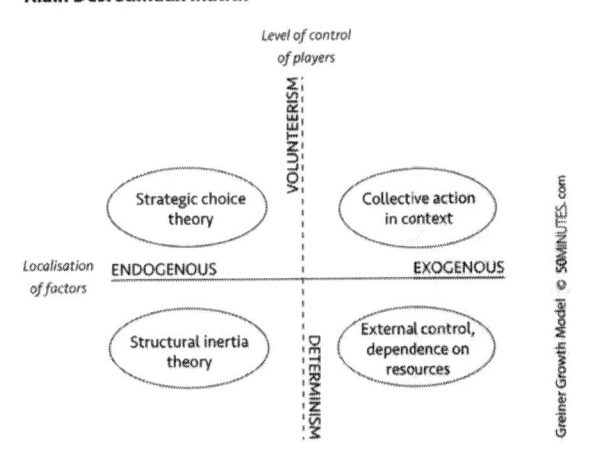

```
                        Level of control
                          of players
                               │
                      VOLUNTEERISM
                               │
       ╭─────────────╮         │       ╭─────────────╮
       │  Strategic  │         │       │  Collective │
       │   choice    │         │       │   action    │
       │   theory    │         │       │  in context │
       ╰─────────────╯         │       ╰─────────────╯
                               │
Localisation   ENDOGENOUS ─────┼───── EXOGENOUS
 of factors                    │
                               │
       ╭─────────────╮         │       ╭─────────────╮
       │  Structural │         │       │  External   │
       │   inertia   │         │       │  control,   │
       │   theory    │         │       │ dependence  │
       ╰─────────────╯         │       │ on resources│
                               │       ╰─────────────╯
                          DETERMINISM
                               │
```

The author uses the dimensions of 'level of control of players' (with a distinction between 'determinism' and 'volunteerism') and 'localisation of factors' (distinguishing the 'endogenous' and 'exogenous' factors of change; some theorists consider that the environment is not only the motor of change, but also the element of selection in organisations).

Desreumaux's matrix provides an overview of the main theories relating to the pace of organisational change.

- **Determinism.** The main characteristics of the movements linked to determinism are the organisation's capacity for inertia and the powerful role of the environment in changing its structures. Indeed, the environment acts as a selection tool for organisations that have not developed their flexibility, and therefore their ability to adapt to change. In this school of thought, the change is endured – by both employees who may, for example, find themselves laid off overnight, and by companies that cannot ensure financial balance. The historical and cultural dimensions, the natural human resistance to change, fear of the unknown, etc. are considered to be major obstacles to the reorganisation of the company. This neo-Darwinian view tries to show the limits of organisations' ability to adapt. According to one radical view embodied by the American sociologists Michael T. Hannan and John H. Freeman (1977), leaders have no control over the environment, while the less deterministic view supported by Jeffrey Pfeffer (specialist in organisational behaviour, born in 1946) and Gerald R. Salancik (organisational theorist, 1943-1996) in 1978, attributes a symbolic role to leaders during times of change.

- **Volunteerism.** The volunteerism movement is characterised by the ability of the participants to create a dynamic of change within the organisation. The motor of change here comes from the proactive role of executives who have the ability – and will – to change the organisation. Its fate is in the hands of the executive and those who have power. The main representative of this school of thought is John Child (management and organisational theorist, 1972). Organisational change is perceived as an instrument controlled by the executives, which has been the subject of strategic proactive anticipation, carried out on a gradual and continuous basis. The strategic and organisational power is based on the executives' willingness to change and their ability to be recognised as legitimate: this kind of executive is now described as an 'inspirational leader'. The trend of the strategic choice theory includes the theories of strategic planning by Gerry Johnson (professor of strategic management, 1987) and Alain-Charles Martinet (French professor of management sciences and business management). According to these two authors, the pace of change can take a revolutionary direction because of the leader's ability to impose deadlines for change within the organisation. Change, and consequently the transformation of social structures, is the result of continuous interaction between different individuals (collective intelligence that allows new solutions to be considered). It can be understood as "a repetition of the formulation of objectives, development, modification and interaction between actors"[1] (Giordano, 1995). However, there is no fixed sequence and it is difficult to predict or identify periods of crisis in the structure of the organisation.

Development of the organisation

In general, it is considered that four phases mark the development of the organisation: the stable and continuous phase, the growth phase without profound change, the phase of uncontrolled change and the phase of profound transformation of the organisation.

---

1. This quotation has been translated by 50Minutes.com.

Organisational growth

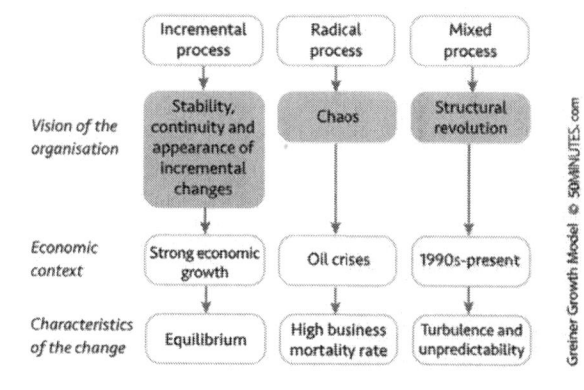

	Incremental process	Radical process	Mixed process
Vision of the organisation	Stability, continuity and appearance of incremental changes	Chaos	Structural revolution
Economic context	Strong economic growth	Oil crises	1990s-present
Characteristics of the change	Equilibrium	High business mortality rate	Turbulence and unpredictability

Greiner Growth Model © 50MINUTES.com

- **Stability and continuity.**
- **Appearance of incremental changes:** during this period, continuous changes allow the organisation to evolve without disrupting its entire structure. The core determinants of the organisation mainly consist of the company's history, its culture and the existing organisational structure. Organisational change is mainly initiated by endogenous factors. The growth phases were described as phases of revitalisation by the Canadian academics Henry Mintzberg and Frances Westley in 1992. In the example developed by Desreumaux, this corresponds to the period of economic growth between 1945 and 1973.
- **Chaos.**
- **Structural revolution:** the revolutionary processes of organisational change often correspond to phases of high pressure from the external environment which drive

organisations to evolve at a rapid pace at the risk of disappearing. The organisation is then pushed to the limits of its ability to accept change. For Desreumaux, these phases emerged with the economic upheavals partly linked to the oil crises of the mid-1970s. They correspond to phases involving a questioning of business models, the fundamentals of organisation management and the core structure of the organisation. The latter is characterised by strong resistance to change from individuals and groups of individuals.

To move past this revolutionary phase, which Mintzberg and Westley (1992) referred to as a 'turnaround period', organisations will need to focus primarily on the management of two key elements, namely the crisis and the emergency. At this point, they need to destroy the past to build the future.

RESISTANCE TO CHANGE

In times of crisis, change can be perceived by individuals as a dramatic event. If communication is not clear, they may feel threatened, fear uncertainty and demonstrate their spontaneous opposition (for example through strikes). Resistance to change is a natural reaction from individuals who seek to protect themselves and in this way defend themselves against any questioning of the balance and stability of the organisation that may endanger their own function and/or legitimacy. Many theorists, including Jeffrey Pfeffer and Gerald R. Salancik, explain the mechanisms of resistance to

> change (psychological and social blocking mechanisms in response to uncertainty, etc.).
>
> Connie Gersick (specialist in organisational behaviour, 1991) stresses the importance of taking into account the history of the company in order to analyse the limits of its capacity for change. Furthermore, according to Nils G.M. Brunsson (Swedish economist, 1982), the process of revolutionary change is characterised by a change in outlook from the organisation, which creates uncertainty, demotivation and prevents the process of change from being incremental.

INCREMENTAL APPROACHES TO THE LIFE CYCLE

As we have seen, this Darwinian approach is inspired by biology: the organisation is seen as a living organism and growth is viewed as a natural phenomenon. From this perspective, organisational change involves a series of cumulative incremental changes. The organisation can accept the change as long as it is limited, while significant changes are the result of the unnoticed accumulation of small modifications. This theory defines the traditional vision of change as a gradual and incremental process, structured around logical sequences called phases. The main advocate of this theory, James B. Quinn (1980), believes that change is the sum of many small events which all influence each other.

The life cycle theory is relatively old and is very widely used in managerial literature. In some cases, it may be applied more to organisational changes than to strategic changes.

Mintzberg and Westley observed in 1983 that the life cycle of an organisation is structured around five phases. The first phase is the stage of development, embodied by a visionary leader who sets objectives. The second phase is the stage of stability, characterised by the planning of the organisational structure, the implementation of procedures and the structuring of the organisation. This is followed by the stage of adaptation, which is marked by minor changes to the organisational structure and strategy, unlike the stage of struggle. The latter forces the organisation to find a new strategic direction. Disorder, challenges, power games and a questioning of the current structure are then observed in the organisation. The stage of revolution includes changes that affect the strategy, culture, structures and individuals in the company. Mintzberg is interested in incremental change and recognises the existence of periods of abrupt, short and intense changes within the organisation.

LARRY E. GREINER'S GROWTH MODEL

To describe the history of company development, Larry E. Greiner (1972) suggests identifying indicators from the organisation's past that could be crucial to its future success.

Greiner believes that it is important to know the history of the company in order to identify key success factors and economic performance over time. He argues that external market opportunities determine the strategy of a company, which, in turn, determines the structure of the organisation. This structure is central to the future growth of the company.

According to him, every organisation passes through five well-defined phases during its existence. Each phase is characterised by a gradual change, followed by a transition crisis or a brief period of revolution. It is the resolution of this crisis that allows the company to move onto the next phase.

Greiner growth model

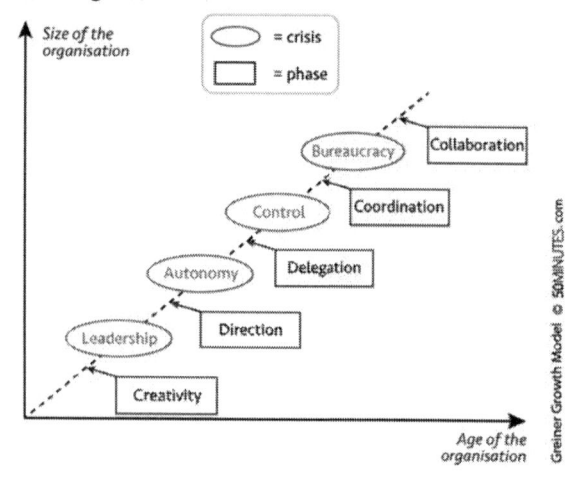

Creativity phase

This first phase corresponds to the launch of the company in a growing market by founders who are often technicians or entrepreneurs, not necessarily leaders or even managers.

Communication within the organisation is frequent and informal, the founders and initial employees do not count their hours, and they are generally happy with modest salaries. The primary motivation is a successful project launch. Their responsibilities are not always clearly defined, they each have several different roles to play and they complete their daily challenges with enthusiasm, often through collegial decision-making mechanisms: they take an active part in the construction of the organisation. The risk at this stage concerns the commitments and departures of members of the organisation (the concept of *affectio societatis*), because it does not take much to unbalance the new structure.

> ### *Affectio Societatis*
>
> This Latin term refers to the relationship between people participating jointly in the capital of a company: together, they invest, share decision-making, share the benefits and risks, etc. Most importantly, *affectio societatis* ensures a certain harmony, which logically should last as long as the company is active. Unfortunately, this is not always the case.

This situation leads to a **leadership crisis**. This occurs when the company, having grown and prospered, must restructure its operations in terms of the production of goods and services, accounting, human resource management, etc. according to the principle of 'specialisation of functions'.

The founders cannot reasonably have all the necessary skills and, according to Greiner, are unable to motivate new employees in the same way as the initial team. Furthermore, they may not really be effective, professional managers and could lack the ability to grasp complex management decisions.

The solution to this crisis is to hire experienced managers who know how to implement the functional structures required. However, this operation comes with risks, as the founders and initial employees may be tempted to keep the original spirit and informal character of the organisation (desire to retain power, self-esteem crisis caused by recognising their limits, etc.).

Direction phase

An individual has taken power and is directing the organisation, allowing it to continue its growth in a more formal environment and to focus on different activities, such as marketing and production. Financial incentives start to appear in order to motivate individuals.

However, there comes a time when the products and processes become so numerous that it is impossible for a single person to manage everything in one day. Sometimes there is not enough time; other times, the flow of information (products and services) to process is too large. As a result, the organisation enters a new period of crisis: autonomy. The **autonomy crisis** is linked to the need to create new structures based on delegation, but also to funding problems related to growth.

The solution to this crisis involves not only a restructuring of the organisation based on the delegation of leadership responsibilities to other members of the company, but also the entry of domestic and/or foreign capital in the organisation.

Delegation phase

The solution to the autonomy crisis leads to the delegation of power from senior management to middle managers. These managers are free to react quickly to opportunities and threats from new products, markets, competitors, technologies, and customer desires and expectations. In this way, the organisation continues to grow.

The people who inject capital do not necessarily run the

company themselves. In most cases, they appoint an agent to represent them and ensure the efficient use of their capital.

This delegation may then lead to a **control crisis**. The chief executive, who wants to continue to solve the fundamental problems of the organisation on their own, finds it difficult to let go. However, the structure of the organisation has become too large for a single leader. Thus, out of pride, many founders unwittingly bring about the downfall of their organisations.

The solution to this crisis requires thoughtful delegation, involving the creation of head of department positions and new offices (departments or subsidiaries). To move forward, it will be necessary to clearly redefine the objectives, tasks and responsibilities of the new leaders and support them in their new assignments.

Coordination phase

Growth continues with business units (departments or subsidiaries depending on their legal status) separated and reorganised into groups of products, services and resources. Ideally, the objectives are shared by the entire company, while the different departments, which also have their own aims, enjoy relative autonomy.

Bureaucracy becomes so significant that costs negatively impact the growth of the organisation. By growing in this way, administrative formalities obscure the primary mission of the organisation. A such, this phase can lead to a

bureaucracy or red-tape crisis, characterised by a loss of flexibility.

To overcome this crisis, the company will need to establish a new culture – focusing on the vision and key tasks of the company – and introduce a new, more flexible, adapted and motivational structure.

Collaboration phase

In the interests of reducing costs and maximising profits, the direction and coordination phases are driven by a new, inspirational and motivational leadership, encouraging the organisation to refocus on its priorities. Promotions, job rotations, and training allow people to excel at work. This phase ends with an internal growth crisis. More broadly, Greiner suggested that growth by collaboration may cause a future crisis, but this remained undefined in 1972.

Future developments

Recently, Greiner added a sixth phase to his original model. He suggests that further growth will only come from outsourcing (developing partnerships with complementary organisations) the organisation's non-core activities.

This sixth phase, which allows growth through extra-organisational solutions, has a number of major advantages:

- a refocusing of the company's core competencies on its core business;
- a reduction in the size and complexity of management (downsizing);

- cost containment (fewer fixed costs relating to staffing and more commercial costs, which may be impacted by the competition);
- quality assurance (the service provider wants to maintain its position);
- greater flexibility for the company, which can change its upstream (supplier) and downstream (distribution) partners depending on its own development strategies.

INTERPRETATION OF THE BUSINESS DEVELOPMENT SCHEME

Every organisation experiences periods of relative stability and periods of crisis. The people, structures and procedures that seemed suitable when the company had reached a certain size or age are no longer suitable when the organisation grows and matures. Management, aware of the past of their organisation, can therefore predict the upcoming crisis, prepare for it by taking appropriate measures for the stage of development that has been reached, and in doing so turn a critical situation into the starting point of a new growth phase.

Not all organisations have gone through these five phases yet. Some, if they become stable at a given size and complexity, may well remain indefinitely in the corresponding phase. Only the European and especially the American giant companies are currently in the last phase of the Greiner Growth Model. However, any organisation that develops should experience these successive periods of calm and crisis, with the speed with which they pass from one phase to another depending on the pace at which the company and its industry are developing.

In the case of a startup (an innovative company with great potential for development which requires significant investments to finance its rapid growth), if the entrepreneur wishes to make their idea a reality and offer the product or service on the market, they should have not only financial resources, but also the management skills necessary for the launch, development and sustainability of the business. The development process of a startup can be broken down as follows:

- the birth of an idea and the search for partners and/or colleagues;
- the setting up of the project in an unfamiliar, and the information and promotion phases;
- public interest in the product or service offered and the beginning of inventory management and supply problems;
- delegation of authority to the experienced managers following the development of the company;
- the company becomes 'too large', leading to bureaucratic problems that prevent the development of the company; if no change is made to the strategy, this can lead to its decline.

The correct use of the Greiner Growth Model allows leaders to anticipate the next steps and ensure the sustainability of the organisation, knowing that startups usually enjoy four to eight years of continuous growth without major economic problems or serious internal disorder.

LIMITATIONS AND EXTENSIONS

LIMITATIONS AND CRITICISMS

The aim of the Greiner Growth Model is to warn business leaders about the likely existence of crises that their company will face over the course of its growth. However, this theory has its limitations and has faced a number of criticisms:

- Firstly, although it is true that many organisations usually start with unsophisticated organic structures and end up with very sophisticated structures, it would be unreasonable to claim that all organisations necessarily go through each of these phases. Some businesses stagnate, regress or skip steps, while others are bought out by larger companies or go bankrupt.
- Secondly, this scenario of company growth remains too theoretical. To date, no study has accurately identified the critical thresholds where crises are triggered. In other words, this model is more of a framework for analysis than an operational tool.
- The Greiner Growth Model sheds no light on the determinants of change or the processes of change themselves. Moreover, it does not explain the causes of failure, the underlying reasons for change or the way that crises develop.
- The model does not allow users to analyse the phase that follows maturity, which is the stage that most current businesses are at.
- Finally, the author does not take into account the inte-

ractions between the different parts of the organisation or the randomness of the pace of change in his analysis.

RELATED MODELS AND EXTENSIONS

The punctuated equilibrium model

This model draws on the historical dimension by granting the leader a limited role in managing change. In this way, it is similar to the volunteerism school of thought, in that it considers most systems to have limits in terms of acceptable change. Beyond these limits, the growth of the company undergoes a fundamental reorganisation. This is contrary to the model created by Greiner.

The thinkers behind the punctuated equilibrium model were Elaine Romaneli (professor of strategic and entrepreneurial management) and Michael L. Tushman (strategic management specialist) in 1983. They state that an organisation experiences long periods of stability interspersed with periods of strategic reorientation that are traumatic for the company and its stakeholders. They characterise the core structure of the company according to the five dimensions of the company's values:

- products;
- markets and technologies;
- distribution of power in the organisation;
- organisational structure;
- nature and type of control.

The main advocate of the punctuated equilibrium theory

is Connie Gersick, who tries to confirm the applicability of this theory in the fields of management and biology, on different levels of analysis: individuals, groups of individuals and businesses.

Other extensions

In order to analyse the operational processes of organisational change in detail, the financial expert David Marsh (born in 1952) has developed a theory of change that is focuses on the everyday life of the organisation.

According to Andrew Pettigrew (professor of strategy and organisation at the University of Oxford, born in 1944), change should not be viewed as a specific moment between two periods of stability, but as a constantly present element that is more visible in times of crisis. For the author, the process of organisational change can be understood by looking at company culture and policy. He highlights the fact that organisational change is the formalisation of a gradual process, which is not visible or planned.

In addition, Henry Mintzberg (1992) considers there to be a consensus stating that generalisations are less valuable than the highlighting of cases, circumstances and contexts, where hypotheses are confirmed. Change comes from the higher levels of the organisation and is implemented by its lower levels.

PRACTICAL APPLICATION: KODAK

In January 2012, a crisis shook the world of photography when a leading camera manufacturer, Kodak, declared bankruptcy. However, everything had started off well for the Eastman Kodak Company.

CREATIVITY PHASE

Following research carried out by its founder George Eastman (American industrialist, 1854-1932) the Kodak group applied for a patent on the method and apparatus for the production of emulsion plates (photographic support for achieving quality photos) in 1885. With their slogan "You press the button, we do the rest", the famous Kodak brand appeared for the first time in 1888, when the first cameras using photographic film were launched in the United States. From that point on, the company was recognised as innovative: it marketed and popularised cameras using photographic film and folding pocket cameras across the world.

This growth phase led to the leadership crisis. With many factories and thousands of employees around the world, William G. Stuber (American manager, 1864-1959) replaced George Eastman as the head of the Kodak group and remained in that position until 1934. Several other experienced managers then followed him.

DIRECTION PHASE

By 1960, Kodak had nearly 80 000 employees. The exponential growth of the company continued with many inventions, including the digital camera developed in 1975 by the American engineer Steve Sasson (born in 1950). This product was marketed poorly or not marketed at all, for fear of harming the lucrative photographic film market, which Kodak dominated. For many observers, it was precisely this digitisation that would later cause the collapse of the multinational company. With sales exceeding $10 billion in 1981, the company was known not only for cameras, but also for the use of images in the fields of leisure, telephones, science, entertainment and commerce.

In order to solidify its influence, Kodak partnered with the *Compagnie Générale des Établissements Pathé Frères Phonographes & Cinématographes* owned by Charles Pathé (French pioneer of the film and recording industries, 1863-1957). This association resulted in the Kodak-Pathé company and would be behind several film productions.

The company continued to invest in research and development and therefore employed several engineers, but also several levels of management. This created a divide between management and the research laboratories, resulting in some unfortunate strategic decisions. The managers did not allow some revolutionary innovations (CCD image sensors, digital X-rays, digital photography, etc.) to be marketed out of fear of jeopardising the high margins from the sale of photographic film.

Kodak experienced an autonomy crisis: many engineers left the company to market their inventions elsewhere with the consent of their former employer.

DELEGATION AND COORDINATION PHASE

Despite a slight decline, the company's growth continued thanks to considerable financial resources (for each dollar of Kodak photographic film sold, research received five cents).

A control crisis was now unfolding: a relatively laissez-faire attitude took hold in the laboratories; the commercial services favoured research based on products rather than on technology or consumer needs; discussions and decisions on the marketing of innovations took months, wasting valuable time. Sometimes, sales representatives who had rejected an innovation without analysis would ask researchers to develop it a few months later (red tape crisis).

To resolve this control crisis, Colby H. Chandler was appointed CEO of Kodak in May 1983 and remained in the position until June 1990. He was responsible for a redefinition of management tasks and functions. The solution to the red tape crisis would only be visible after bankruptcy in January 2012.

COLLABORATION PHASE

Confined to the lucrative photographic film market for many years, Kodak entered the digital market late and was unsuccessful with its line of EasyShare products. From 2007, the company experienced financial difficulties. In response, it decided to sell its patents, restructure its departments, forge new partnerships, split from several associates around the world and abandon its traditional business (photographic film) to focus more on modern technologies (digital photography and cinema).

Unfortunately, all these efforts did not bring the expected results. In January 2012, the company was placed under the protection of US bankruptcy law. A year after filing for bankruptcy and closing 13 factories, Kodak started anew with 8 500 employees. Technically ready, the company developed applications (still in the prototype phase) to return to centre stage. However, they would need several innovations and inspirational and motivational leaders for the timid recovery to last.

At the moment, Kodak is offering a unique line of inkjet printers. These new-generation printers have a scanner that can serve as a photocopier and allow for printing at lower costs compared to competitors such as HP or Epson.

Greiner growth model – Kodak

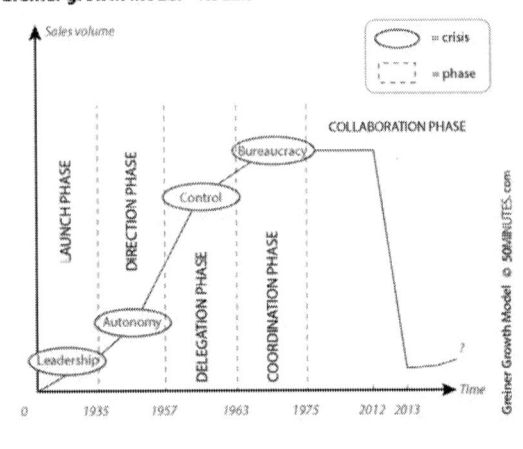

SUMMARY

- Larry E. Greiner has shown that a company experiences alternating phases of growth and crisis over the course of its growth. These periods of change are an integral part of an organisation. To ensure its sustainability, the organisation must incorporate the life cycle concept and make full use of it to derive the benefits and assert itself on the market.
- The five phases of a company life cycle are:
  - creativity;
  - direction;
  - delegation;
  - coordination;
  - collaboration.
- Despite the undeniable parallels between the business life cycle and that of humans, some companies may not experience the last phase of the growth cycle: decline or death.
- Although the Greiner Growth Model is more of a framework for analysis than an operational tool, the punctuated equilibrium model shows that it is possible to go past these approaches in terms of particular cycles of change, particularly with the model created by Andrew Pettigrew.
- Finally, the story of Kodak shows that innovation and change are key factors in the success of a company.

We want to hear from you!
Leave a comment on your online library
and share your favourite books on social media

FURTHER READING

BIBLIOGRAPHY

- Atamer, T. and Calori, R. (1998) *Diagnostic et décisions stratégiques*. Paris: Dunod.
- Barthélemy, J. (1999) L'externalisation : une forme organisationnelle nouvelle. *Actes de la huitième conférence de l'Association internationale de management stratégique*.
- Demers, C. (2007) *Organizational Change Theories: A Synthesis*. Thousand Oaks: Sage Publications, Inc.
- Desreumaux, A. (1996) Nouvelles formes d'organisation et évolution de l'entreprise. *Revue française de gestion*. pp. 86-108.
- Deval, E. and Nury, G. (2009) *La notion de cycle biologique intégrée par le management*. Valence: Institut Supérieur Technologique Montplaisir.
- Gersick, C. (1991) Revolutionary Change Theories: A Multilevel Exploration of the Punctuated Equilibrium Paradigm. *The Academy of Management Review*. Volume 16, pp. 10-36.
- Giordani, Y. (1995) Management stratégique et changement organisationnel : quelles représentations? *Les nouvelles formes organisationnelles*. Paris: Economica. pp. 161-179.
- Gould, S.J. (1990) *The Panda's Thumb*. London: Penguin.
- Greiner, L.E. (1972) Evolution and Revolution as Organizations Grow. *Harvard Business Review*. pp. 37-46.
- Henriet, B. (1999) La gestion des ressources humaines face aux transformations organisationnelles. *Revue française de gestion*. pp. 82-93.

- Lemaire, L. (2003) *Systèmes de gestion intégrés. Des technologies à risques?* Paris: Éditions Liaisons.
- Mintzberg, H., Thomas, J.M. and Bennis, W.G. (1972) *Strategy Safari: The Management of Change and Conflict.* New York: The Free Press.
- Peretti, J.-M. (1998) *Ressources humaines et gestion du personnel.* Paris: Vuibert.
- Perret, V. (No date) *Rythme et processus de changement : processus incrémental ou révolutionnaire.* Dossier Management du Changement et TIC. [Online]. [Accessed 23 December 2014]. Available from: <http://dea128fc.free.fr/CoursA/A2-ManagementChangement&TIC/expo/valery/DEA128FC-Processus%20incr%E9mental%20et%20r%E9volutionnaire.pdf>
- Perret, V. and Josserand, E. (2003) *Le paradoxe. Penser et gérer autrement les organisations.* Paris: Éditions Ellipses.
- Pettigrew, A. (1987) Context and Action in the Transformation of the Firm. *Journal of Management Studies.* 24(6), pp. 649-670.
- Quinn, J.B. (1980) *Strategies for Change: Logical Incrementalism.* Homewood, Illinois: Richard D. Irwin, Inc.
- Reix, R. (1990) L'impact organisationnel des nouvelles technologies de l'information. *Revue française de gestion.* pp. 100-106.
- Romanelli, E. and Tushman, M. (1996) Inertia, Environments and Strategic Choice: A Quasi-Experimental Design for Comparative Longitudinal Research. *Management Science.* 32(5), pp. 608-621.

ADDITIONAL SOURCES

- Mullins, L.J. (2016) *Management and Organisational Behaviour.* Edinburgh: Pearson.

© **50MINUTES.com, 2016. All rights reserved.**

www.50minutes.com

Ebook EAN: 9782806268402

Paperback EAN: 9782806270641

Legal Deposit: D/2015/12603/441

Cover: © Primento

Digital conception by Primento, the digital partner of publishers.

Printed in Great Britain
by Amazon